Introduction

MW00884526

The Photos App

(1st Edition)

© 2017 iTandCoffee

Special Sales and Supply Queries

For any information about buying this title in bulk quantities, or for supply of this title for educational or fund-raising purposes, contact iTandCoffee on **1300 885 420** or email <u>enquiry@itandcoffee.com.au</u>.

iTandCoffee classes and private appointments

For queries about classes and private appointments with iTandCoffee, call **1300 885 420** or email **enquiry@itandcoffee.com.au**.

iTandCoffee operates in Melbourne, Australia.

iTandCoffee
Relax, we'll help you get iT

Introducing iTandCoffee ...

iTandCoffee is a Melbourne-based business that was founded in 2012, by IT professional Lynette Coulston.

Lynette and the staff at iTandCoffee have a passion for helping others - especially women of all ages - to enter and navigate the new, and often daunting, world of technology.

At iTandCoffee, **patience is our virtue.**

You'll find a welcoming smile, a relaxed cup of tea or coffee, and a genuine enthusiasm for helping you to gain the confidence to use and enjoy your technology.

With personalised appointments and small, friendly classes – either at our bright, comfortable, cafe-style shop in Glen Iris or at your place - we offer a brand of technology support and education that is so hard to find.

At iTandCoffee, you won't find young 'techies' who speak in a foreign language and move at a pace that leaves you floundering and 'bamboozled'!

Our focus is on helping you to use your technology in a way that enhances your personal and/or professional life – to feel more informed, organised, connected and entertained!

Call on iTandCoffee for help with all sorts of technology – Apple, Windows, iCloud, Evernote, Dropbox, all sorts of other Apps (including Microsoft Office products), getting you set up on the internet, setting up a printer, and so much more.

iTandCoffee
Relax, we'll help you get iT

Here are just some of the topics covered in our regular classes at iTandCoffee:

- Introduction to the iPad and iPhone

- The next step on your iPad and iPhone

- Bring your Busy Life under Control using the iPad and iPhone

- Getting to know your Mac

- Understanding and using iCloud

- An Organised Life with Evernote

- Taking and Managing photos on the iPhone and iPad

- Travel with your iPad, iPhone and other technology.

- Keeping kids safe on the iPad, iPhone and iPod Touch.

- Make a photo book from your digital photos.

- Staying Safe Online

The iTandCoffee website (itandcoffee.com.au) offers a wide variety of resources for those brave enough to venture online to learn more: handy hints for iPad, iPhone and Mac; videos and slideshows of iTandCoffee classes; guides on a range of topics; a blog covering all sorts of topical events.

We also produce a regular Handy Hint newsletter full of information that is of interest to our clients and subscribers.

Hopefully, that gives you a bit of a picture of iTandCoffee and what we are about. Please don't hesitate to iTandCoffee on 1300 885 420 to discuss our services or to make a booking.

We hope you enjoy this guide, and find its contents informative and useful. Please feel free to offer feedback at feedback@itandcoffee.com.au.

Regards,

Lynette Coulston (iTandCoffee Owner)

Introduction to the Mac
The Photos App

TABLE OF CONTENTS

TABLE OF CONTENTS (cont.)

TABLE OF CONTENTS (cont.)

Introduction

The **Photos** app on your Mac provides a place to manage all your Photos and videos – your 'library' of photos (and videos.)

By importing all photos and videos using the **Photos** app (into your **Photos Library**), it is then possible to view, organise and share them in multiple ways.

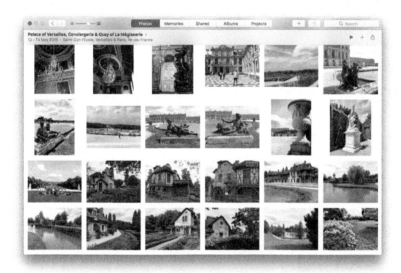

Photos (and videos) can be viewed on a **timeline,** allowing a 'drill-down' to a photo or set of photos based on when the photo was taken – starting first with **Years**, then **Collections** within a Year, and then **Moments** within the Collection. We'll look at this 'timeline' view shortly.

Photos and videos can also be viewed as 'Memories', by places, people and other 'albums', presented in slide shows, used to create photobooks, shared with others via iCloud, and more.

Your other Mac applications can use your photos/videos and albums that are stored in your **Photos** library - for example, when inserting a photo in your email, the search screen allows you to browse **Photos** for the image you wish to include.

It is important to note that, if required, you can make the choice about whether **Photos** 'stores' your photos in the **Photos Library**, or whether it just 'points' to the photos that are stored elsewhere on your computer – or even on an external hard drive.

This will be explained and covered in more detail a bit later.

For those who are familiar with iPhoto and iOS Photos

Moving from the iPhoto app

For anyone who was previously using the **iPhoto** app to manage their Mac's photos, the migration to the new Photos app can be a cause of significant confusion, leaving the user wondering what happened to the iPhoto sidebar, and what happened to all their 'Events'.

Rest assured that neither has been lost.

If you want to see a sidebar again in the Photos app (like that you had in iPhoto), simply go to the menu bar at top and choose

View -> Show Sidebar

This takes away the options from the top centre of the window (refer to the image on the previous page to see what I mean by this) and instead shows the sidebar, providing more information about the contents of the Shared and Albums areas.

To see the Events that were previously in the Library section at the top of the iPhoto Sidebar, look in the **Albums** area.

All of your events are now individual Albums, grouped under a 'Folder' named '**iPhoto Events**'.

For those who are familiar with iPhoto and iOS Photos

So, they have not disappeared – they are just in a different place. Events are no longer used to group sets of photos that you import to the Photos Library.

The Photos timeline (Years, Collections, Moments) has replaced the concept of Events. We'll look at this 'timeline concept shortly.

Comparing Mac Photos to iOS Photos

The Photos app on the Mac has a very similar design as that of the iOS Photos app on the iPad and iPhone. Let's look at what we mean by that. (For those of you who don't have an iPad or iPhone, you may wish to skip this sub-section.)

The image above shows the Mac's Photos app in MacOS Sierra, with a set of options along the top – **Photos**, **Memories**, **Shared** (which may not appear for everyone), **Albums** and **Projects**.

You will see that the iOS 10 Photos app (right) shows the same set of options <u>along the bottom</u> (excluding Projects).

(iOS 10 and Mac OS Sierra versions of Photos have the new Memories option you will not see in iOS 9 or earlier OS X versions.)

The 'Photos' Option –
Viewing a Timeline of your Photos

Let's look first at the '**Photos**' option/view, which offers the same functionality on both the Mac and your iOS device. As mentioned earlier, '**Photos**' gives you a way of viewing your photos <u>on a timeline</u>.

Clicking the **Photos** option at the top the screen (or in the Sidebar, if you have enabled this) will reveal a 'timeline' of your images, grouping them first into 'Years', then 'Collections' within these years, then 'Moments' within the Collections.

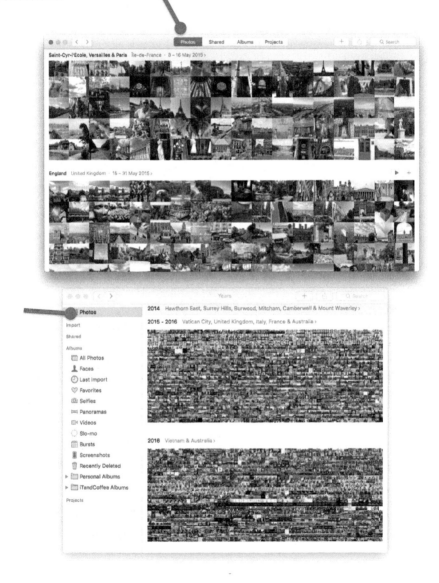

The Photos Option – Viewing a Timeline of your Photos

When you first click on this Photos option, you may find that you are initially viewing the '**Moments**' view – which is the 'bottom' level of the timeline 'hierarchy'.

A **Moment** is a day, or set of days, in which a set of photos were taken. Double-click on any photo in your **Moment** view to view that individual photo.

You can move 'up' a level to the '**Collections**' view (where a collection is made up of multiple 'Moments'), then up further to the '**Years**' view (with each year made up of multiple 'Collections).

Here's another way of thinking about this timeline hierarchy of your photos.

Consider a house (your Photos app) with rooms (Years). One of the rooms (a particular Year) that has couple of wardrobes (Collections).

Open one of the wardrobes (a particular Collection), to find a set of drawers (Moments) inside.

Open one of the drawers (a particular Collection) to view the socks inside.

The photos are the socks in the drawer!. Does that help?

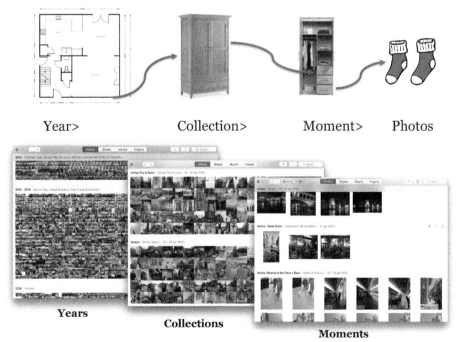

Year>   Collection>   Moment>   Photos

Years

Collections

Moments

The Photos Option –
Viewing a Timeline of your Photos

You can effectively 'drill down' to find the photos you are interested in, starting first by finding the Year in which it was taken.

When you get into the Moments view, double-click click on a **thumbnail*** to view a larger version of the individual photo.

* A Thumbnail is a mini version of a photo, giving you a preview of the photo so that you can decide if that's the one you wish to look at.

The Years View

The 'Years' view shows tiny thumbnails of the set of photos that were taken in a particular Year.

The date stored against the photo is used to automatically put each photo into its applicable 'Year'.

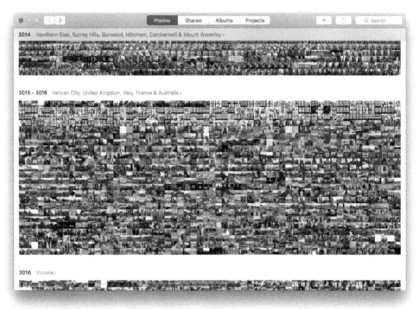

The date will have been assigned to the photo when it was taken, either by your camera, iPhone or iPad. For a camera, this means that the date must have been correctly set at that point in time.

Information like 'date-taken' is known as 'metadata'. Each photo has metadata that tells us when it was taken, which camera took it, perhaps where it was taken and more. We'll look later at how you can view this 'metadata' for a photo, and how you can change incorrect/missing metadata.

The Photos Option –
Viewing a Timeline of your Photos

In the 'Years' view, scroll up and down to view your set of years.

To go to a particular Collection: Click once on a specific Year (anywhere on the group of little photos) to enter that year and view the year's photos in several '**Collections**'.

To go to a particular photo/video: Alternatively, double-click an any mini-thumbnail in the Year view to go directly to that photo.

The Collections View

The Collections view displays slightly bigger 'thumbnails' and shows your images grouped by date ranges and, perhaps, by location and date range.

It is important to note that the 'Place' grouping of the photos will only work if your phone, tablet or camera stored GPS (ie location) information against the photo at the time the photo was taken. We'll see later how this information can be added retrospectively.

Click just once on any **Collection** (i.e. on the area with the small images of the photos) to see the photos from that Collection grouped by **Moments**.

Double-click on any individual thumbnail to go directly to that photo.

To go back to your **Years** view, click on the < at the top left (next to the traffic lights).

The Photos Option – Viewing a Timeline of your Photos

The Moments view

This view gives full thumbnails from a specific place or date (sometimes multiple dates). Scroll up and down to find the image/s that you want to view.

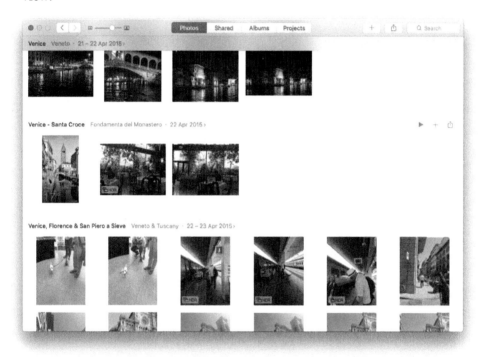

Double-click on any photo's thumbnail to view that individual photo.

In this view, you will also see a 'zoom' slider in the top bar, towards the left (near the 'traffic lights').

This slider allows the size of the Thumbnails to be enlarged and reduced to suit your requirements – handy when you are searching for a photo, or comparing similar photos.

To go back to your **Collections** view, click on the < at the top left (next to the traffic lights).

The Photos Option –
Viewing a Timeline of your Photos

The headings are special!

In each of the **Years**, **Collections** and **Moments** views, you will see 'headings' showing the place and/or date for the group of photos.

Depending on whether your photos in that group have any location information stored against them (which must have been stored at the time the photo was taken, or manually added after), you may see 'place' details in the each header.

If you do see 'place' details in the header above the set of photos, you can click on the header itself.

For MacOS Sierra

In MacOS Sierra, clicking on the location in the heading above the set of photos will bring up a different style screen to that which applied in Yosemite and El Capitan.

A summary of your photos will be shown, with the option to Show All. Click this to see *all* of the photos for applicable to the heading that you selected.

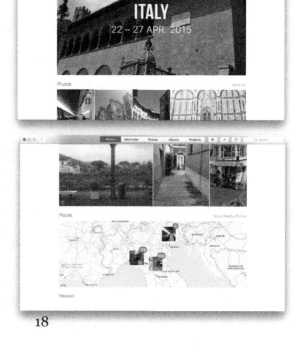

At the bottom of the summary of photos will be a map that shows the various locations where the photos were taken.

Double-click this map to enable further viewing of the photos in 'Map' view.

A map of your photo locations will appear, allowing for zooming in and out on the map

The Photos Option –
Viewing a Timeline of your Photos

the see where photos were taken.

The + and – at bottom right provide the 'zoom in' and 'zoom out' capability.

Choose to view the map in Standard, Satellite and Hybrid view (options at top right of map.)

Then, click on any of the 'thumbnails' shown on the map to view the pictures taken at that place in thumbnail view.

The Photos Option –
Viewing a Timeline of your Photos

Double-click on any of these thumbnails to view the individual image.

To go back a step at any point, just select the < at the top left, next to the 'traffic lights'.

For OS X Yoesmite and El Capitan

Clicking on the Place name in the heading above a group of photos will take you straight to the Map view of your photos, without the intermediate screen.

Viewing individual photos/videos

Getting to a single photo/video

When you are in a view that shows individual photo thumbnails, **double-click** on any image's thumbnail to view the individual photo.

Alternatively, if an item is already selected, press the space bar to view that item.

Then, use the right and left arrow keys on your keyboard to move to the next or previous photo

Returning to previous 'view'

Use the < symbol at top left to go 'back up' to the previous level (eg back to the applicable Thumbnail view).

Enable 'filmstrip' of photos

While in the individual view of the image, click on the symbol to the right of < to enable a 'filmstrip' of photo thumbnails as a

- sidebar on the left-hand side in Yosemite & El Capitan or

- bar along the bottom in MacOS Sierra.

Click on a thumbnail in the side or bottom bar to view a different image.

Click the same symbol to hide the thumbnail sidebar/bottom bar.

Viewing individual photos/videos

View in Full Screen

To view your photo or video in 'full screen' mode, click the green traffic light.

You may first need to choose View – Hide Sidebar if you don't want to see the Sidebar in full screen mode.

To zoom in on a photo, adjust the slider that is to the right of the traffic lights.

Play a video

If the item is a video, you will see a bar of symbols when you bring the mouse pointer over the image on the screen.

- **To play a video:** Click the 'Play' symbol ▶

- **To stop a video:** Click the double bars ||

Your toolbar of options

When you are viewing an individual photo or video, you will see some options at the top right.

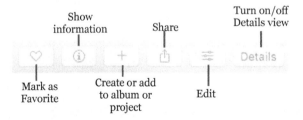

We will look at these options throughout the upcoming sections of this guide, but for now let's just look at the 'Heart' option.

Viewing individual photos/videos

'Heart' your favorites

You may have noticed that the bar of options that is visible when viewing individual photos includes the ♡ option.

The ♡ option allows you to specify certain photos as your 'Favorites'.

Click on this heart to 'Favorite' a photo that you are currently viewing. The photo will then automatically appear in the **Favorites** album.

Any photo that has been set as a 'Favorite' will show a shaded heart. Just click the heart again to remove the photo from your Favorites.

Revisit a Moment

This is something I find very handy, especially when checking for duplicated photos or wanting to check what other similar photos exist for a photo I have put in an album or that appears in my All Photos album.

If you are viewing a photo in a view other than Moments, right-click on it and choose **Show in Moment**.

This will take you straight to the Moments view, with the selected photo highlighted with a blue border.

The Details view

The **Details** view is new in MacOS Sierra.

It shows a special view of the selected photo, including quick access to related photos of people found in the photo, or of the place where the photo was taken.

Click the **Details** option turns this special view on; clicking it again turns this view off.

The look of this 'view' is very similar to the 'Memories' view, described in the next section.

Memories -
New in Mac OS Sierra

The Memories option was introduced to the Photos app by Mac OS Sierra and iOS 10, late in 2016.

Here is how Apple describes this feature:

> *"Rediscover favorite and forgotten moments from deep in your photo library. Memories automatically creates curated collections of your most meaningful photos and videos."*

The contents of the **Memories** area of the Photos app will be chosen for you automatically by the Photos app, from (supposedly) the best photos in the library (although I'm not convinced this is always true!).

You will see 'Memories' like those shown in the screen shot at above right. Just double-click on a particular Memory you wish to view

A summary of the photos in the 'Memory' are shown, with the option to **Show All,** or perhaps play a slideshow of the 'Memory'. (We cover slideshows a bit later in this guide.)

Thumbnails of the 'people' appearing in the 'Memory' are shown, as is a map with the location of the Memory's photos and other 'related Memories'.

24

Memories -
New in Mac OS Sierra

If you like the Memory, you can choose to keep it – by adding it to your Favorites. If you don't like it, just delete it – to stop it appearing again. These options are available at the bottom of the **Memory** view, when viewing an individual Memory.

Add to Favorite Memories

Delete Memory

I must say that I have not made much use of this feature on the Mac yet, but do visit it on my iPad and iPhone, as those devices play the Memory as a lovely pre-made movie.

For further details on the Memory feature, check out the Apple Support article https://support.apple.com/en-au/HT207023.

The Albums View

As mentioned earlier, the Photos app allows for the organising of photos (and videos) by arranging them into **Albums**, or for viewing of photos in standard Albums that Apple has provided for you.

Click **Albums** in the top bar to view your current set of albums. If you have the Sidebar visible, you will see your list of albums there.

If you don't see anything listed in the Albums area of your sidebar, hover the mouse pointer over the word Albums so that the word **Show** appears, then click this **Show** option to reveal the list of albums. (The same action then allows you to 'hide' the list of Album again.)

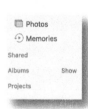

Lets look first at the standard 'albums' that are provided by Apple - these are the albums that cannot be deleted and that will appear automatically if there are any photos that belong in that Album.

In some of the below descriptions, we will mention something called iCloud Photo Library – a relatively new service from Apple (since April 2015) that, at the moment, can cause a lot of confusion and issues.

Depending on whether this service is turned on, and on which device/s it is turned on, different behaviour is applicable in the Photos apps on Apple mobile devices and on the Mac.

For the moment, we will concentrate on the situation where iCloud Photo Library is NOT enabled. Further discussion on this feature is included later in this guide.

The Albums View - Your Standard Albums

All Photos

The **All Photos** album is a special album that shows all of the photos and videos that have been added to your Photos Library, listing them in 'date added to the library' order.

This means that the order of the items in All Photos will usually be quite different to that you see in the Photos view, which will always order items by 'date taken'.

Favorites

Favorites shows any photos you've marked as being favourites by clicking the heart icon at the top when viewing the individual photo.

If you are not using iCloud Photo Library, Favorites you have chosen on your iPad or iPhone are separate to those on your Mac. This means that, even if you have 'hearted' a photo on you iPhone, it won't automatically appear in Favorites on your Mac (or your iPad, for that matter).

(iCloud Photos Library users will find that syncing of Favourites DOES occur between devices.)

Faces *(Yosemite & El Capitan)* or **People** *(MacOS Sierra)*

This special album splits photos into groupings according to facial recognition. We'll cover this a bit later in this guide.

Places

This album is new in MacOS Sierra and shows your photos on a map, for any photos that have location information stored with them.

Zoom in and out on this map to 'split out' your photos by their location. It is a great way of seeing all the places you have been!

Videos

As you can probably guess, the Videos album shows all the videos that are in your Photos Library.

The Albums View - Your Standard Albums

Last Import

This album shows the photos that were last imported to your Mac from a Camera, SD Card, iPhone or iPad, or another Import method – see later in this guide for methods of importing photos you your Photos library.

This set of photos is replaced each time an Import is performed, so remember to create an album of your Imports at the time it is done (that is, if you are keen to be able to return to this set of photos later).

(Last Import does not include any new photos automatically added by iCloud Photo Library or added by My Photo Stream.)

Selfies

This album shows any photos in the library that were taken with the front camera of your iPad or iPhone (or the Facetime camera on your Mac).

Panoramas, Slo-Mo, Time Lapse and Bursts

These albums show any photos that you took with your iPad/iPhone and using the corresponding feature from that device. You do not have to put photos/videos into these albums – they magically appear there, based on information that is stored about the photo that is stored as something called 'metadata'.

My Photo Stream

Depending on your Photos app's 'Settings', you may see the **My Photo Stream** album in your Albums list.

This album contains the photos that have been 'streamed' to your device via iCloud. Refer later in this document for more information about My Photo Stream.

(If iCloud Photo Library is turned On, you will not see the My Photo Stream album – even if the feature is enabled.)

Screen Shots

This album shows any 'screen shots' taken on your iPad or iPhone.

Screen shots on your iPad and iPhone are pictures taken by pressing the sleep switch and home button simultaneously on the iPad or iPhone. This takes a photo of whatever is currently showing on the device's screen and

The Albums View -
Your Standard Albums

stores this photo in your Photos app on that device, in the Camera Roll (or All Photos if iCloud Photo Library is enabled).

Hidden

This album is for showing photos you have chosen to keep hidden from the casual observer!

By right-clicking on a photo and choosing 'Hide', you hide the photo from other views and make it only visible in the Hidden album. It will not be seen in Moments, Collections, Years and Memories views, but _will_ still be visible in Albums (and in the Hidden album).

Recently Deleted

Just as it sounds, the Recently Deleted album holds photos you have decided to 'trash'.

The Photos App retains deleted photos and videos for about 30 days (sometimes up to 40 days); in case you make a mistake and need to retrieve them.

Photos in this album show the days remaining before permanent deletion.

To permanently delete the photos from this album (and thereby free up their allocated storage), just choose **Delete All** (which will be at top right) when viewing this Album.

.

Selecting Photos

Quite often, you will have the need to select more than one photo – for example, to select a set of photos to add to an album, to delete, to put in a slideshow, to share and more.

There are several ways to select photos:

Select a single photo

Just click on a thumbnail, or double-click to open that photo.

Select multiple random photos:

Multiple random photos can be selected (and unselected) in thumbnail view by **holding down the Command Key** as you click on each item in the view.

Select inclusive range of photos:

An inclusive range of photos can be selected by clicking the first photo in the range and then, as you click the last photo in the range, **holding down the Shift key**.

Select all photos:

Click any image in the thumbnail view and then choose **Command-A** (select all).

Unselect selected photos:

If you have selected multiple photos, you can then **unselect** certain of these photos by **holding down the Command Key** as you click the photo/s

Selected photos are indicated with a blue border.

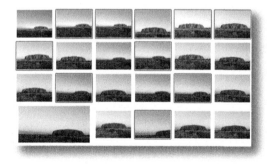

Refer to this page whenever we talk about selecting photos later in this guide.

Deleting photos

Understanding 'Delete' vs 'Remove'

Photos can be **Deleted** a few different ways.

But before we discuss these methods, we need to first discuss the difference between 'Removing' a photo from an Album and 'Deleting' a photo.

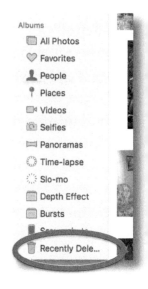

Always make sure you check the message that appears when you are deleting, too confirm if you are actually 'deleting' or 'removing'. What do I mean by this?

If you are looking at photos in one of the standard albums (All Photos, Videos, Selfies, etc) **or from the Photos timeline,** and you choose to Delete any of these photos, you will be **deleting** the photos from the Photos Library.

They will go into the **Recently Deleted** album, and be permanently deleted after 30 days (approx.).

If you are looking at a set of photos that are in an Album that you have created (we'll look at creating your own albums shortly), you will just be 'removing' the photo/s from that Album, but leaving them in the Photos library and in any other Album that you have added them to. The same applies to photos in a **Memory.**

(That is, unless you specifically choose the 'Delete' option described by the second bullet point below, where you right-click on photo/s and choose **Delete** instead of **Remove**.)

If you are going through a process of deleting unwanted photos, it is best to be viewing one of the standard albums (All Photos, Videos, Selfies, etc) or the thumbnails in the Moments or Location views, not viewing them in an Album you created yourself.

Ways to Delete

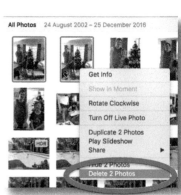

1. When viewing thumbnails of many photos in one of the standard albums or in the Photos view, select one or more photos (refer earlier) and choose ⌘-**delete** **(Command-Delete)** on the keyboard.

2. Right-click (or two-finger-click) on the selected photo/s (refer earlier for methods of selecting multiple photos) and choose

Deleting Photos

the **Delete** option from the list of options that appear.

3. When viewing an individual photo, press **Delete** key (or ⌘–**delete** (**Command-Delete)).**

Command-Delete **will not** ask you to confirm the deletion.

If you are removing photos from an Album you created, you will not be asked for confirmation if you use methods 1 or 3.

Otherwise, methods 1 and 3 will request confirmation.

As mentioned earlier, deleted photos and videos will be moved to the **Recently Deleted** album.

If a photo was incorrectly deleted, go to the **Recently Deleted** album, select the photo or photos, and choose **Recover** (top right).

Photos 'removed' from an album or Memory will still be available in the Photos library, and can be re-added to the album/Memory if required.

Some hidden space gobblers to delete

If you have a newer iPhone or iPad – one that is capable of taking 'Bursts' (rapid-fire photos taken by holding down the white dot, instead of just tapping that dot), you may find yourself with quite a few 'bursts' of several photos, instead of just the single photo that you want.

Visit the **Bursts** album to find and eradicate these extra photos.

In the example shown here, I can see that there are three sets of 'bursts' in my Bursts album.

What I really want to do is choose the best of the each set of photos and delete the rest.

To do this, double-click to view one of the 'bursts'. At top right of the photo is 'Make a Selection'. Click this to view the full set of photos in the burst.

Deleting Photos

Along the bottom shows a ribbon of the photos in the burst.

Click each photo in this ribbon in turn, and choose to 'tick' or 'untick' it – to show that you do or don't want to keep that photo.

Once you have chosen which photos you want to keep from the burst, choose **Done** at top right.

If you have only elected to keep some of the burst's photos, you will be asked what to do with those that you didn't select.

Usually, you will want to click **Keep Only Selection**, so that the unselected photos are moved to the Recently Deleted album (and eventually deleted).

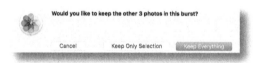

A Handy Tip if you make a mistake when deleting

Don't forget that, in most cases, you can **Undo your last action** – for example, restore incorrectly deleted photos – by simultaneously pressing the two keys.

⌘-z (Command-z)

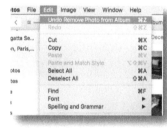

The Edit menu provides the same 'Undo' option, in case you forget this keyboard combination. It even shows you exactly what the ⌘-z combination will 'Undo'.

Also available in the Edit menu is the **Redo** option, should you decide that you need to reverse the 'Undo'.

The exception to this is if you Delete your photos from the Recently Deleted album. This **cannot** be undone.

Organising your Photos - Find your People

The **People** album (called Faces in El Capitan and Yosemite) offers a great way of viewing all the photos of a particular person, using facial recognition to discover and group photos.

The first time you visit the People album in Mac OS Sierra, your Photos app will show a set of thumbnails that represent sets of photos that have been determined as showing the same person.

By clicking on the number below the picture, you can allocate a name to the person – ideally using the name of someone stored in your Contacts (although you can just assign any name you like).

Your most important people can be dragged to the top (above the line) to set them as your 'Favorite' people.

If you use the same name for a different thumbnail, you will be asked if you wish to merge with the other group of photos for which you assigned the same name.

Simply name each of the thumbnails shown or choose Delete after highlighting an unwanted 'person'.

When this is done, click the **Add People** box to identify more people. A screen showing a heap of suggestions will appear.

Organising your Photos - Find your People

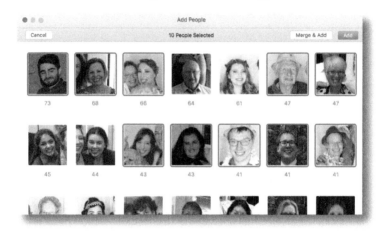

Using the Command key, click each 'face' that you want to add to the main People screen. Click **Add** (top right) to finish this selection and addition.

Once they are on the main People screen, name each one in turn (as described above).

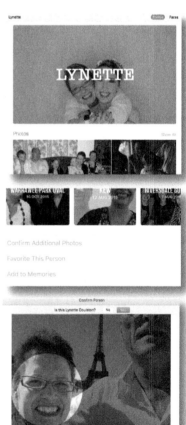

For each identified 'Person', double-click the thumbnail on the main People screen to view the 'already-matched' photos of that person, shown as a 'Memories' style screen with lots of ways of viewing photos of the person.

Scroll down that screen to see some additional options at the very bottom.

Click **Confirm Additional Photos** to look for more photos of the same person.

You will then be taken through a series of photos, and asked to confirm if each one is (or is not) the applicable person. Click 'Yes' if the photos IS of the person, and 'No' otherwise.

Choose **Done** at top right to finish, or wait until you have exhausted all the possible potential matches.

Organising your Photos - Creating an Album

Many of us end up with a huge number of photos on our Mac.

While the timeline functionality in the Photos view, and the Memories, People, Places and other features of MacOS Sierra allow us to find the photos we are looking for, the best way to organise those photos is to create your own Albums that contain the photos for a particular occasion, holiday, person, place or other grouping.

Albums offer a great way of showcasing your photos to family and friends, and a great way of organising your images so that you can find them when you need them! A photo can appear in multiple Albums that you create.

There are two key ways to create albums

1. Create the album, then add photos to it or

2. Select a group of photos, then choose to create a new album.

We'll look at each of these methods.

Method 1: Create an album, then add the photos

To create an 'empty' album, choose

File -> New Empty Album.

Then, type in the **Album Name** for your new album and click OK.

You can then either

- Drag photo thumbnails to the album in the sidebar or

- Select photos and use the + symbol at the top right.

We'll look at how to add photos to an existing album shortly.

Organising your Photos - Creating an Album

Method 2: Select photos, then create a new album for those photos

Using the method described in **Selecting Photos** earlier in this guide, select one or more photos that you wish to include in the new Album.

Then, use one of the following methods to create the new album.

    1. File –> New Album or

    2. Choose + symbol from top right and choose Album

In either case, you will see a screen like that below – enter your Album Name, and choose OK to complete creation of the album.

Organising your Photos - Adding Photos/Videos to an Album

Adding photos to an existing album is very easy, especially if you enable your Sidebar, so that you can see your list of Albums on the left-hand side.

Use Drag and Drop

One way to add photos to an existing album is to simply select one or more photos and drag them across to on top of the name of the Album.

A blue bar will appear across the Album Name to show that it is the one that is selected. If you let go, the selected photos will 'drop into' that album.

Use the + symbol

Adding photos to an existing album is almost the same as creating a new album.

Simply select the photos that you wish to add, then choose the + symbol from top right and, once again, choose Album.

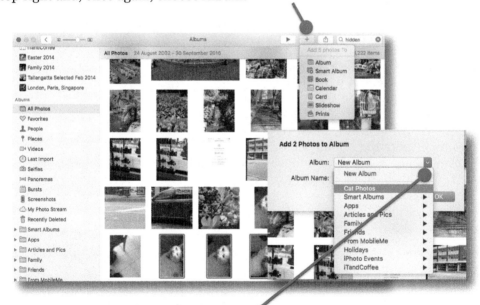

This time, click on the 'down-arrow' symbol next to the word 'New Album' and find the album you wish to add to. Click that album name (in my case, **Cat Photos**) and then click 'OK'.

The photos will be added to the selected Album.

Organising your Photos - Managing Albums

Renaming an Album

If you want to rename an existing Album, just right-click on it in the Sidebar and choose '**Rename Album**', then enter the new name for the Album.

Or, if viewing the albums as 'Thumbnails', just click on the name underneath the thumbnail, and change.

Rearranging Albums

Albums can be listed in the order that you choose. In the sidebar, or just click and drag the Album to the required location. A blue line (see below) will show the position where the Album will be moved – just release the mouse or trackpad to 'drop' the Album to that position.

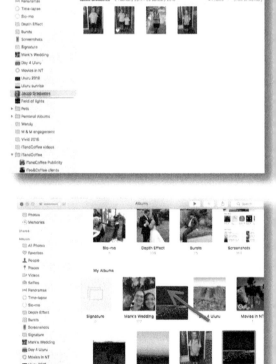

If you are viewing the albums as thumbnails, just click and drag the Album thumbnail to the required position

Organising your Photos - Managing Albums

Deleting Albums

Deleting an Album that you have created will simply remove the Album and its corresponding grouping of photos.

The photos in the album will still exist in the Photos library and in any other Album in which they have been placed.

If you want to delete an Album, just right-click on it in the Sidebar or on its thumbnail and choose '**Delete Album**'

Sorting Photos within an Album

Photos within an album that you create can be sorted manually, or can be sorted automatically by title, or date-taken.

Just right-click on the album name and choose Sort. Then choose the desired sort option as shown in the below image.

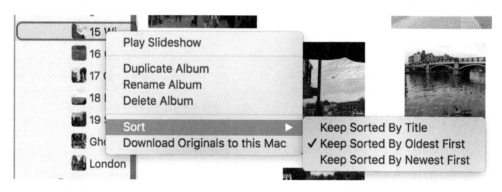

If you would like to manually sort your photos, just ensure that no options are ticked in the Sort option. To 'untick', just click on the option that is ticked.

If none of these 'automatic sort' options are ticked, you will be able to drag photos into the order you require. In this case, photos added to the album will appear at the end of the album's photos, ready to be re-arranged.

Organising your Photos - Managing Albums

Grouping Albums into Folders

Over time, you may find that you end up with a very long list of Albums – and need to be able to group these Albums together, and perhaps 'hide' the albums you are not currently using.

In the Photos app, it is possible to set up a whole structure of folders and sub-folders for storing Albums.

To create a Folder, simple choose **File->New Folder.**

Give the folder a name, and then drag Albums or other folder/s on top of this new folder to move them to that folder.

You will see the album (or folder) is moved into the Folder – showing inside the folder's the thumbnail, or in the sidebar by clicking the ▶ on the left of the folder name.

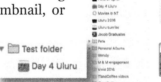

Creating a Folder Structure

To create folders within folders, simply drag one folder on top of the other.

You can create a multi-level folder structure, helping to keep all those albums easy to find.

When using the Sidebar, you can also right-click on any Folder and choose New Folder to create a folder within that folder.

In the example on the right, I can easily find the holiday photos that I took in Italy when we travelled to Europe in 2015.

Organising your Photos - Managing Albums

Renaming Folders

Renaming and re-arranging folders can be done in the same way as described above for Albums.

To rename, just right-click on the folder name and choose **Rename Folder**.

Alternatively, select the folder then click again on the name to get into 'edit' mode to change the name.

Deleting Folders

Right-clicking on the folder name also gives the **Delete Folder** option.

Deleting a folder will simply remove the folder and any folders and albums it contains.

The photos that were in the folders albums will still exist in the photo library.

Rearranging and sorting Folders

Drag folders around to manually re-order.

To automatically sort folders (or folders/albums within folders), right-click on the folder name or on the **Albums** heading to choose the **Sort** option.

Choose to sort by **By Name**, **By Newest First** or **By Newest First**.

Sharing Photos and Videos

The Photos app allows the sharing of the photos (and videos) from your Photos Library, using email, Messages, iCloud, Facebook. You can also add them to Notes, set an image as your Desktop picture, and more.

You can choose to share an individual photo or video, or several at once (limits apply in certain cases though).

Videos can be shared in email and text messages, and even on YouTube.

Sharing photos or videos

Choose one or more photos (or video) using the method described earlier in **Select Photos**

Then click   at top right to uncover your set of 'Share' options.

Click on the required 'Share' option from the list shown.

Depending on what Apps you have on your Mac, you may be able to add additional 'share' apps by clicking on the **More...** option.

Emailing photos

Choose the **Mail** option in share to send one or more photos via email.

If you send multiple images, just make sure that the email you are creating is not too big to send.

The size of the email is shown in **Message Size.**

If the email with images is over 500KB in size, you will be given the option to send the images as a smaller size.

Sharing Photos and Videos

The file size of the photos that you send can be adjusted using the **Image Size** field. Just click on this to see the various sizes that you can send, and to choose that which will apply to the current email. The Message Size will

adjust when you change the Image Size.

This image size setting will then be 'remembered' for the next email that you send.

This means that, if you adjust the size to Medium when sending a set of photos via email today, then the next time you create an email with photos, they will be automatically sized as Medium.

This can then be changed if you require a different sizing next time around – and will again be 'remembered.

Sharing Photos with others via iCloud

A set of photos can also be shared using your iCloud, by setting up **Shared iCloud Albums.**

We will cover this in more detail later in this guide, as it gets us into the more complex territory that is iCloud!

Viewing your photos as a Slideshow

The **Slideshow** option allows your Photos app to automatically cycle through an album (or even all your photos/videos), showing your images/videos.

You can have fancy 'transitions', and can even play your show with music – your own music, if you so desire.

The Slideshow option is available when you are viewing thumbnails of photos in an Album. It is the arrow symbol.

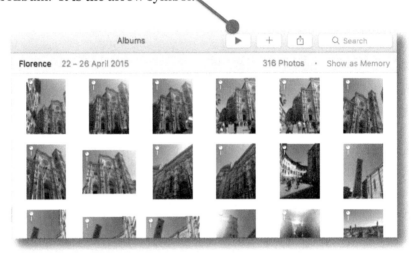

You will also see the same arrow if you hover the mouse pointer over the set of photos in a Moment or Collection. It will appear above the Moment/Collection, on the right-hand side. Look out for it in other places too – for example, in a Memory.

Viewing your photos as a Slideshow

Clicking this arrow will result in some options for presenting your slideshow – the 'theme' and music.

The **Theme** will determine the 'style' of the slideshow – try out each theme to work out which one suits. A preview of the theme (and the default music that will play with it) will show in the small window above the theme names.

If you have any music in your iTunes library, you will be able to choose a single track to play with your Slideshow (instead of the default music).

Just choose the **Music** option at the top to see the music that you can choose from. Only music that is stored on your Mac can be chosen for your slideshow.

When you have finished setting up your Slideshow, just click **Play Slideshow** at the bottom to enjoy your slideshow!

You will also find the '**Play Slideshow**' option when you right-click (or two-finger-click) on an album or folder.

Creating a more customised slideshow

It is also possible to create a 'saved slideshow' Project, which allows for the re-ordering of photos, different transitions, text slides and captions and more.

The best way to create a Saved Slideshow is to first create an Album that contains the photos that you want to include in your Slideshow.

Then, just click on the Album in the sidebar or as a Thumbnail, and choose +, then Slideshow.

This will create a slideshow in the same name as the Album, and including all the photos that are in the Album.

There are lots of additional options for then customising this Slideshow 'project'. Why not give it a go!

Getting Photos into your Photos Library

Import Photos from an iPhone, iPad or iPod Touch

Using the cable that came with the Apple mobile device, connect the device to the USB port on your computer.

If the i-Device is not on, turn it on. Make sure you unlock it with your passcode.

If the i-Device pops up a message asking if the device should 'Trust' the computer, confirm the **Trust** option.

The **Photos** app should open automatically. If it doesn't, click the **Photos** app in the Dock to open it.

The photos and videos on the device will be analysed, and you will be shown which are already on the Mac, and those that are not yet on the Mac.

Do one of the following:

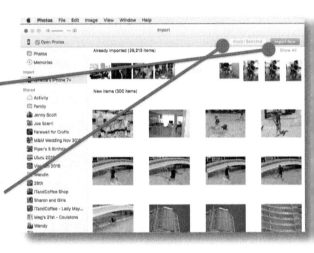

- To import all new photos from your camera, click the **Import New** button.

- To import only some photos, use the methods described earlier to select multiple photos, and then click the **Import Selected** button.

If the Photos app did not open automatically when you plugged in the i-Device, tick the '**Open Photos for this Device**' option at the top to ensure that the device automatically opens next time the device is plugged in.

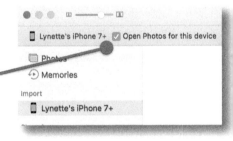

After the import process is finished, disconnect the USB cable.

47

Getting Photos into your Photos Library

Import photos from a digital camera

Using the cable that came with the camera, connect the camera to the USB port on your computer or, if your Mac has an SD card slot, you can insert the SD card into that slot.

If the camera is not on, turn it on, and make sure it's set to the correct mode for importing photos. For information on which mode to choose, see the instructions provided with your camera. If your camera has a "sleep" mode, make sure it's disabled or set to a time increment long enough to allow your images to download.

Open the Photos app, if it's not already open or it does not open automatically.

The import process is then the same as described for your Apple mobile device.

Import photos from internal/external storage

If you have photos saved on your computer's hard drive (if, for example, you scanned photos or downloaded photos from an email), you can import them into Photos.

The same applies if the files are on a USB Flash drive (USB stick) or an external portable hard disk drive.

Importing can be achieved in a few ways

- With both the Finder and Photos windows visible, drag one or more photos or a folder of photos from the Finder onto the Photos option in the Photos app's sidebar, or onto the All Photos album, or onto an album that you have created.

  If duplicates are detected, you will be asked if you want to continue importing the photos or to 'skip' duplicates. Choose 'Apply to all duplicates' if you wish your choice to apply to all imports.

- Drag one or more photos or a folder of photos from the Finder to on top of the Photos icon in the dock.

- In Photos, choose **File->Import...**, then find and select the photos you want to import, then and click **Review for Import**.

Getting Photos into your Photos Library

The second two options will give the standard 'Import' screen that applies for mobile device and camera imports.

Choose whether to store photos in the Photos Library when Importing

Before you import the photos from your Mac or external storage device, you can choose whether you want your photos actually stored in your Photos Library.

This is done in the Photos Preferences.

> ➢ Go to **Photos->Preferences-> General**

> ➢ Tick or untick the '**Copy items to the iPhoto Library**'.

If you choose not to copy the photos to the Photos Library, they will be left in their original location and just referenced by the Photos app. In this case, the 'source' of the photos must be available when you use the Photos app. If that source is an external storage device, the device must be plugged in and available.

If you choose to **Copy items to the Photos Library**, you can then choose later to delete them from the original location (unless you really want to keep them as a backup in that other location).

Save to Photos directly from an email, Message, or web page

A photo received in a mail message can be directly exported to Photos

'Right-click' (or two-finger-click) on the photo (or select more than one by holding the Command key as you click the photos) and choose the **Export to Photos** option.

Getting Photos into your Photos Library

The same applies for photos in your Messages – except the option is **Add to Photos Library**

Similarly for web pages, photos you find in Safari may also be able to be saved to your Photos library.

Right-click (or two-finger-click) on a web page's photo, and (if it is available) choose the **Add Image to Photos** option.

You will then be able to find any photo that you add in this manner as the last in the **All Photos** album.

They will appear in the **Photos** timeline according to the date and time information recorded against each photo.

Note. Only photos that you give you the 'Import' review screen will go to the **Last Import** album initially.

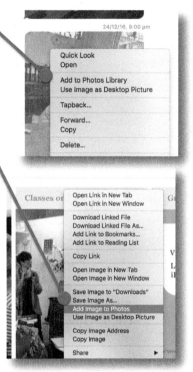

Where do my photos 'live'

The photos you see in your Photos App are held in a special file that usually lives in your Pictures area on your Mac.

The special file is called **Photos Library.photoslibrary**

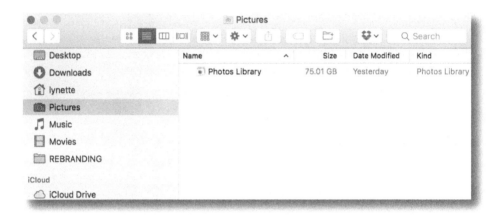

Whenever you open the Photos app in the Dock, it will look for this special file and show you its contents.

Double-clicking on the Photos Library.photoslibrary file will also open that library using your Photos App.

Storing your Photos Library elsewhere

In saying that Pictures is the usual location of the Photos Library, this library does not have to 'live' in this particular location.

In fact, your Photos Library could be stored anywhere on your Mac, or even on an External Hard Disk Drive.

More than one Photos Library

You can even have more than one **Photos Library**, and can open any alternative Photos Library by simply double-clicking on the **Photos Library** file in Finder.

Where do my photos 'live'

Your Photos app will 'remember' which library was last opened, and will open the same one again if the Photos app is selected from the Dock.

If you do have more than one Photo Library, only one library can be the 'main' library used as your 'system' library and by your iCloud.

In **Photos -> Preferences**, the **General** option shows the location of the **Photos Library** you are currently using.

If the current library is not the 'system' photo library, you do have the option to make this alternative library into the main library by choosing 'Use as System Photo Library' (which will be available if you are currently viewing an alternate photos library).

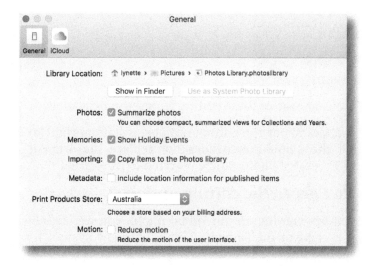

Be very careful about changing this though! If you have been sync'ing with iCloud, you will be messing around with this – something you may not wish to do!

Editing Photos

What sort of Editing is possible?

Quite often, the photos that we take can be made so much better with some minor (or major!) adjustments.

The following editing capabilities are provided by the Photos app on your iPad and iPhone:

- Enhance
- Rotate
- Crop
- Filters
- Adjust
- Retouch
- Red-eye
- Extensions

We will look at each of these editing features in turn shortly.

Before we talk about the editing options, it is important to note that the edited photo does not replace the original photo. Your edited photo can be reverted to its original state at any time.

How do I get to the editing options?

When you are viewing an individual photo, you will see the option at the top right of the screen. This is the new symbol for '**Edit**', which applied prior to iOS 10.

Editing Photos

Just select any of the editing options to make the necessary changes to your Photo, and choose **Done** when you have completed editing.

Once you have applied any of these editing options, you will notice the **Revert to Original** option appears at top right, to allow you to go back to your un-edited version of the photo at any time.

Enhance

Enhance can provide a quick-fix for a not-so-great photo.

It balances the darks and lights and improves the contrast and brightness.

Just click on the **Enhance** option to see what a difference it makes.

Rotate

You will sometimes find that your photo has the wrong 'orientation', so is not able to be viewed in full screen mode, or requires you to stand on your head to view it!

Click on the **Rotate** option to rotate the image 90° anti-clockwise. Keep clicking **Rotate** until your image is oriented correctly.

Crop

The **Crop** feature of Edit mode allows you the change the borders of the photo – to cut out part of the photo or zoom on the main area of interest.

It also allows for the straightening of your photo.

Click on **Crop** and you will see a border appear with 'tabs' at each corner.

You will also notice a 'wheel' on the right that can be used to adjust the angle of the photo.

Editing Photos

In the example below, I drag the borders so that the snow in the picture is more prominent. I first see the photo on the left below. By the time I finish my cropping, I see the result on the right.

If I am finished, I choose the **Done** option at top right to save my changes.

One thing to consider when cropping is whether you want to maintain the same '**Aspect ratio**' for the image – which means keeping or changing the shape and proportions.

To adjust this, just click **Aspec**t, which is on toward the bottom right of the crop screen.

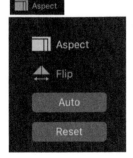 Choose to required Aspect. **Original** will set the proportions based on the original size (ie if it was a standard 4x6 photo, the shape will be adjusted accordingly).

For the photo shown above, here is the result of choosing **Original.**

I can then drag the photo around within the new framed area to adjust the positioning of the features of the photo within the frame.

At any point if I want to undo all the cropping and straightening that I have done, I can choose the **Reset** option.

If I am happy with my cropping, I can choose **Done.**

Editing Photos

Filters

Filters provides a way of changing the colours and tones of your image with a number of special effects, such as black and white, faded, a 'polaroid' look, and a few others.

Click on **Filters** to see the different options available.

To choose a different effect for your photo, just click on one of the filters.

If you like that 'look' and wish the save the photo with this new effect, click **Done** at the top right.

To put your photo back to its original, unfiltered look, choose the **None** filter at the top of the list.

Adjust.

The Adjust option allows the colour and brightness of your photo to be adjusted.

Simply drag the vertical bar to adjust the lighting level or colour level up and down.

If you want a black and white photo, drag the bar to give the required black and white effect.

For more 'granular' adjustments, choose the 'down-arrow' that appears whey you position the cursor over the word 'Light', 'Color' or 'Black & White' to get further 'sliders'.

Here is the set you get for 'Light', allowing more advance photo editors to play with various effects in their photos.

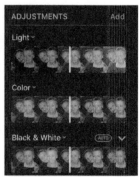

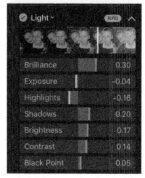

Editing Photos

Extra 'adjustment' option can also be added by choosing the 'Add' option at top right.

I'll leave those of you who are advanced photo editors to have a play with these options and work out what they do!

I won't go into these more advance photo editing techniques and features in this particular guide!

Retouch

Retouch allows you to remove unwanted objects or defects from your photo. It can even help smooth out those wrinkles! Have a play with this option to get the hang of it!

Below is an example of a photo that I have quickly and easily 'retouched' to remove the dog and the school badge.

Selecting the **Retouch** option provides the set of options shown on the right, and some instructions about how to remove unwanted 'things' from your photo.

In the example above, I set the slider to about midway (to give a medium sized circle), then first 'Option-clicked' on the green couch area above the dog.

This set the replacement 'dot' that would be used when I clicked and dragged over the dog. I had to click and drag a few times to get the required effect.

I then did the same thing with the jumper, option-clicking on a blue patch of jumper then clicking several times on the jumper logo to remove it.

Editing Photos

Red Eye

We've all seen those photos taken with a flash, where the person in the shot looks like they are possessed – with red eye/s.

Your Mac allows you to remove red eyes from photos really easily.

Photos that have any faces will include an extra option in the Edit list, called Red-eye. This option does not appear if the Photos app does not detect any eyes!

Just click on **Red Eye** and you will see some additional options, as shown on the right.

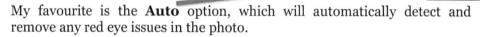

My favourite is the **Auto** option, which will automatically detect and remove any red eye issues in the photo.

If you are not happy with the Auto results, adjust the slider and click on each of the problem eyes to see if you get a better result.

Hopefully your subject won't end up looking too demonic!

Extensions

For most Mac users, clicking on the extensions option will only give options 'Markup' and 'More...'. If you have any photo editing apps on your Mac, the More option will allow you to access any 'extensions' (ie a set of tools) that those apps provide for the Photos app.

Markup is a very handy option (added in MacOS Sierra) that allows you to 'draw on' an image, add a text box, and perform various other 'markup' operations. Choose **Save Changes** when you are done.

Viewing and changing information about your Photo

It can be very useful to view the information about your photos, to find out things like

- The size of your photo
- When it was taken
- What device took it
- Location

It is even possible to adjust date, time and location data stored against a photo. All of this information is known as the 'metadata' of the photo.

Let's look at the ways you can view and edit this 'metadata'.

The Info option

While viewing an individual photo, you will see the ⓘ option in the set of options at the top right. Click this symbol, or right-click (two-finger-click) on any photo and choose **Get Info**.

The metadata associated with the photo or video is shown in a separate window, including a map with the photo location (if this information is stored against the photo's).

If any 'faces' are found in the photo, you will have the chance to allocate a name to each face (for any that don't yet have a name).

Also available are some fields that can be added and edited by you - Title, Description, Keywords, faces.

Including these pieces of additional information about your photos and videos provides further ways of viewing, searching and organizing your photos and videos

Identify Faces in a photo

Choosing the + option in the Faces section will add a new 'circle' to your

Viewing and changing information about your Photo

photo, one that can be placed over the face of an unidentified person, and then allocated a name. (We cover the People option separately in this guide).

Add or change a photo's location

Location information can be added later to any photo or video - very useful if you forgot to turn on Location Services on your iPhone or iPad, or if your camera does not have GPS capability.

In the Info view, click **Assign a Location** and then start typing the location – city, street address, country or attraction. You will see suggestions from Maps appear – select the one that applies to your photo or video.

This will then allow your photo (or video) to be shown on a map, in the Places album, and in other areas of your Photos app that show maps.

Changing a Photo's date and time

In some situations, it is desirable to modify the date/time information stored about a photo (or a video).

To do this, select the applicable photo (or several photos) and then choose (from the main menu)

Image -> Adjust Date and Time

This will show a screen that allows the adjusted time to be set, as well as the time zone applicable to the photo.

It is important to note that the original details of the photo are not lost when this is done, and can be restored at any point if required.

Trimming Videos

The videos that you stored in your Photos library can be very easily trimmed, to remove unneeded footage from the start or end.

When the cursor is hovered over the video, you will see a bar with various symbols.

In particular, you will see the 'settings' symbol. Clicking on this will reveal a set of options, one of which is the Trim option.

Click trim to see a film strip like that shown below, with a yellow band around it.

Just drag the left edge of the bar to the right and/or the right edge of the bar to the left to trim the start and end.

Once you are finished, choose Trim to complete the trimming process. Easy!

If you decide that you want your untrimmed video back, just click the ⚙️ symbol again, and choose the **Reset Trim** option (which will be available if there has been a trim performed previously).

Duplicating photos and videos

On occasion, it may be necessary the take a copy of a photo – perhaps before you apply some edits, so that you can see the edited and unedited version of the photo side by side.

First select one or more photos using the method described earlier in the guide.

When one or more photo/s is selected, you will find the **Duplicate** option as follows:

- Choose **File->Duplicate n Photo(s)**

- Right-click (or two-finger-click on the selected photo) and choose **Duplicate n Photo(s)**

The duplicated photo/s will keep the same date/s, time and location information as the original/s.

Depending on what view you are in, you may not see the duplicated photo/s 'side-by-side' with the original/s.

If you are in the **Moments** view, you should see them side-by-side.

But the **All Photos** view will show the duplicate/s as the 'last created' photo/s – so at the end.

Albums and Folders can be duplicated too

If you ever need to duplicate an album or folder that you have created, just right-click (two-finger-click) on it and choose the **Duplicate** option that appears in the list.

Searching for photos

When you are viewing thumbnails of photos (ie you are not viewing an individual photo), there will always be a **Search** field showing at the top right.

This Search feature allows for searching for photos/videos based on a wide range of search criteria.

- Place

- Person/Face

- Date or Date range

- Keyword, Title, Description (if you have any of this user-specified data recorded against your photos)

- Category - eg Christmas Tree, Tree, Water, Dog, Cat, (new in OS X Sierra)

On the right, you can see what I get if I type the letters 'cat' into my search field.

Having found a set of photos that match your search criteria, you can then quickly create an album containing the photos that match.

Such an album can then be used as part of the rules for a Smart Album (see next section).

Organising your Photos - Smart Albums

We have previously covered how to create your own Albums of photos – and how to go about adding photos to those albums.

These standard albums only contain the photos that you choose to put into the album.

There is another type of album that can be created, one that can determine its contents automatically based on a set of 'rules' that you define.

These are called **Smart Albums**.

Creating a Smart Album

As an example, you could set up a Smart Album that includes all videos that were taken in a date range.

To create a Smart Album, choose **File -> New Smart Album.**

Alternatively, click the + symbol and choose **Smart Album.**

You will see the following screen, where the rule or rules for your Smart Album can be defined.

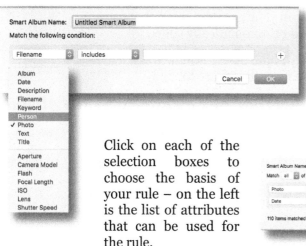

Give your Smart Album a name in the first field, then choose the first condition.

Click on each of the selection boxes to choose the basis of your rule – on the left is the list of attributes that can be used for the rule.

Organising your Photos - Smart Albums

In my case, I will set up my first condition to look for 'photos' that have type 'movie', and the second condition to look for items with a 'date' in the past 6 months.

(I chose the + symbol on right of the first conditions to create a second condition. If I need to remove a condition, I use the -.)

I have also set my rule to require that 'all' of the conditions are true for a photo to be included (instead of 'any').

Once I choose OK, a new Smart Album will appear in my Albums area, with the chosen name.

Viewing Smart Albums

Smart Albums are listed in your set of Albums, and are indicated by the symbol on the left side

The contents of the Smart Album are determined by the rule, so it is not possible to 'drag' or manually add photos to the Smart Album.

The Smart Album's contents will change dynamically based on the photos that are currently in your library – those that meet the Smart Album's rule/s will be automatically added.

If a photo that was previously in the Smart Album is deleted, it will be automatically deleted from the Smart Album.

Sorting, editing, duplicating, and deleting a Smart Album

Various options relating to the Smart Album are available by right-clicking (two-finger-clicking) on the album.

Choose **Edit Smart Album** to change the albums rules.

The name can also be changed in the same way, by choosing the **Rename Smart Album** option.

Sort the contents of the Smart Album using the Sort option. And, of course you can **Duplicate** and **Delete** the Smart Album.

Exporting Photos

On occasion, you may find it is necessary to export a set of photos from your Photos app – say to a USB stick or external hard drive.

Exporting of a selection of photos can be achieved as follows:

- Select your photos
- Choose File –> Export

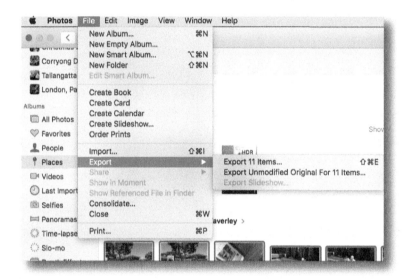

- You will see there is the option to '**Export xx Items ...**' or to '**Export unmodified Original for xx items...**'.

- The first option will export the 'modified' version of your photo/s, including any edits, face allocations, adjustments to date/time and location, and any title/description/keyword additions.

- Each photo will retain the 'date and time taken' metadata associated with each photo/video, **BUT** the 'date created' and 'date modified' showing in Finder for each image file will be the date and time that the export occurred. This can be very frustratintg!

- If you want to keep the date/time that the photo/video was taken in Finder, you will need to choose the second option - '**Export unmodified Original for xx items...**'. The disadvantage of this option is that any edits you have applied to your photo will not be included in the exported photo/s and video/s.

Exporting Photos

For the **Export xx Items ...** option you will see the screen on the right.

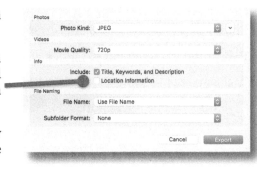

If you want to include Location information with the exported photos, tick the 'Location Information' option.

Choose **Export** when you are ready to choose the disk location for the exported items.

You will then see the standard Finder 'Save' screen, that allows you to choose where to save your exported photos/videos.

You can even create a New Folder in which to store the items.

Once you have chosen the location, click the **Export** button.

A slightly different, simpler export screen appears if you chose the second option, **Export unmodified Original for xx items...**

Select **Export**, to again get the Finder 'Save' screen and complete the export process of the original versions of the photos.

Handy tip for exporting a selection of photos

If you have a random selection to export, it is best to set up an Album first.

Once your album is complete, click on a single photo or video 'thumbnail', then press **Command-A** to select all photos in the Album

Then choose **File -> Export**, and follow the steps described above.

Remember, if you Export the 'unmodified' photos, your photos keep date information

Sorting out all those Duplicates

It is certainly not unusual to find yourself with lots of duplicate photos in your Photos Library.

Unfortunately, Apple doesn't provide any built-in capability to search for duplicates.

The best way to search for duplicates manually is to use the Photos 'timeline' view, where you will see any situations where you have the same photos side-by-side.

But this can be very tedious.

Another option is to purchase a 3rd-party product that allows you to sort out all those duplicates a lot more quickly.

I have purchased a product called **PhotoSweeper,** available in the Mac App Store. This has served me very well in my quest to rid my library of the duplicates that creep in there on a regular basis.

Of course, there are many other products that do the same thing, and this guide is not seeking to recommend any one product.

Your best bet is to Google reviews of products that manage duplicated photos on a Mac – and make your own assessment and purchase.

Melbourne readers can always visit iTandCoffee for one-on-one assistance with resolving duplicate photos.

Photo Books

The Photos app allows for quick and easy creation of Photo Books that are produced and delivered to you by Apple.

These photo books are really are lovely – although they are not the cheapest photo book on the market by any stretch! And there are other tools on the market that are offer a lot more flexibility in your book's design.

To create a book of photos using the Photos app:

1. Select the photos you want in the photobook.   The best way is to first create an Album for your Photobook

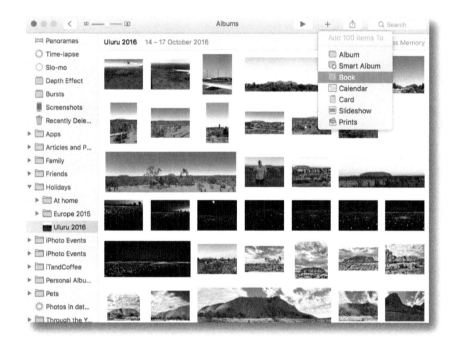

2. Click on the Album you wish to use and choose the + button at top right.

3. Choose **Book** from the drop down menu.

4. The window updates to show book sizes and prices.

5. Select the required size/style.

69

Photo Books

6. Select your Theme – click the one you want

7. Choose **Create Book**

8. Your photos will be automatically added to your book.

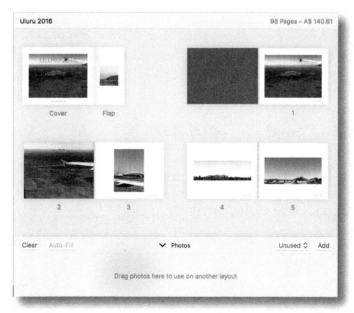

Photo Books

9. If you want to choose your own positioning of photos, choose the **Clear** option at bottom left and do the positioning of photos yourself.

We won't go into detail on how to create a photo book in this guide, as this is covered by a separate class and guide offered by iTandCoffee.

But here are just a few tips

➢ The theme of the book you choose will determine what page styles are available to you. Some styles only allow very basic layouts, while others allow more flexibility including text etc.

➢ Click the  symbol at the top right to show the 'Layout Options' pane (see right). This allows for the layout and backgound colour of each page to be chosen.

➢ If you are finding that that theme you chose is not giving you sufficient options, try a different theme. Choose the Book symbol at top right and choose **Change Theme.**

➢ Extra photos can be added to the book – just choose 'Add' at bottom right.

➢ When you are finished, choose **Buy Book** at top right.

➢ Complete the steps to order your book – you will need to sign in with your Apple ID and follow the instructions provided.

To create a card or calendar, or order prints:

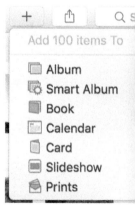

The same steps apply to other products offered by Apple. Choose the + symbol after selecting an album or a set of photos, then choose the desired product.

Now let's talk about Photos in iCloud

There are three aspects of iCloud that relate to your photos and videos. These are

- iCloud Photo Library

- My Photo Stream

- iCloud Photo Sharing

For any of these options to be available in the Photos app, your Mac must be using iCloud.

To check if you are signed in to iCloud, go to

 System Preferences -> iCloud

Here is a summary of what each of the three iCloud photos features offers. We will then cover each of these areas in further detail in the next few sections of the guide.

iCloud Photo Library   Stores all your photos in iCloud and allows each of your devices to view and manage this same set of photos and Albums.

Extra iCloud storage may be needed to store large libraries, and devices that can't fit entire library will need internet access when viewing any photos. (Note. Windows computers can also use iCloud Photo Library.)

My Photo Stream   Allows streaming of photos (not videos) between your iCloud-enabled devices, including Windows computers, whenever those devices are connected to Wi-Fi. My Photo Stream photos areonly held in iCloud for 30 days, and only last 1000 stored on mobile devices. My Photo Stream DOES NOT offer permanent storage of your photos in iCloud.

iCloud Photo Sharing   Allows creation of albums in iCloud, that can be then shared with other people. These Shared Albums are separate to your iCloud photo library – so deleting a photo from your library will not delete from any Shared iCloud Album (and vice-versa).

72

iCloud Photo Library

iCloud Photo Library was introduced in about April 2015. It provides centralised storage of all your photos in iCloud, and allows the viewing and updating of the 'library' in iCloud from any devices connected to that iCloud account.

The great benefit of iCloud Photo Library

Photos and albums are synchronized between all devices that are connected to the iCloud Photo Library – meaning that albums can be create on an iPhone, iPad and Mac, and be visible then on all other devices.

It also means that photos deleted on one device are also deleted on other devices.

For many people, this offers a great solution to storage of their photos.

The disadvantages of iCloud Photo Library

The problems start when your Photos library is a large one.

iCloud Photo Library offers only an 'all or nothing' solution to storage of your photos on each device. This means that, if iCloud Photos Library is turned on, the device will show EVERY photo and video that is in the library.

If your library is big, it may not fit on your mobile devices.

In this case, your device will store 'cut down' versions of your photos – versions that are 'blurry' and can only be viewed properly once they are downloaded from your iCloud.

In this case, you need internet access to view your photos, and have to endure a delay before you can see full resolution versions of your photos and videos.

This can result in unexpected mobile data usage, and great frustration at not being able to view photos when there is no internet.

iCloud Photo Library currently does not offer the option to choose which photos/albums are available on which devices, leaving those who use it with the "all or nothing" choice. (This is the situation at the time of writing this document – hopefully it will change soon.)

If your Photo Library does not fit on a device, the photo storage must be 'optimised'.

Added to all this is the cost of storing all your photos in iCloud. If your Photos library is large, you will be looking at a higher iCloud subscription cost of $4.49 per month for 200GB or perhaps $14.99 per month for 1TB.

iCloud Photo Library

Should you use iCloud Photo Library?

At the time of writing this guide, iTandCoffee's recommendation is that you don't set up iCloud Photo Library unless you are fully aware of the implications.

If iCloud Photo Library has been accidentally enabled, it can be tricky to undo.

This guide will not seek to cover the topic of 'undoing' iCloud Photo Library, should you decide to stop using it.

If you require information about this topic, contact iTandCoffee at enquiry@itandcoffee.com.au.

My Photo Stream

My Photo Stream is part of iCloud – a feature that you can choose to enable on each of your Apple devices.

*(**Important Note.** If you are using iCloud Photo Library, you won't need to use My Photo Stream unless you have a device that is not yet using iCloud Photo Library.)*

My Photo Stream's purpose is to allow streaming of photos (not videos) between your Photo Stream-enabled devices.

If your iPad or iPhone has this feature turned 'on', photos you take on your that device will be uploaded to iCloud for 30 days. A Wi-Fi connection is required for this upload to occur.

If the feature is turned 'on' in your iCloud settings on the Mac, photos found in your **My Photo Stream** in iCloud will automatically download to your Mac when it is connected to the internet.

When you open your Photos app, the already downloaded Photo Stream photos will then bevimported into your Photos Library. They may take a little while to appear.

The **My Photo Stream** album in the Photos App shows that photos that appear in your Photo Stream. *(Note. The My Photo Stream album is not present in Photos if iCloud Photo Library is turned On.)*

To turn on your **My Photo Stream** in Photos on your Mac, go to **Photos -> Preferences -> iCloud -> My Photo Stream.** Ensure this option is ticked.

An important thing to remember is that, while any photos imported to you Mac via My Photo Stream will remain on you Mac until you delete them, the My Photo Stream album on the iPhone and iPad will only ever hold a maximum of 1000 photos. Older photos will disappear from the My Photo Stream album on those devices once you reach 1000.

iCloud Photo Sharing

Sharing your photos using iCloud

A set of photos can be shared using your iCloud, by setting up **Shared iCloud Albums.**

Shared iCloud Albums allow you to share an album of photos with other iCloud users, and with other 'non-Apple' people.

I use iCloud Shared Albums all the time to share photos of trips, family events and more.

Those who share the album with you can like, comment, or even add more photos to the Shared iCloud Album.

For this option to be available, you must ensure the following setup has occurred:

- Sign in to iCloud on your Mac - this is done in **System Preferences -> iCloud**

- Turn 'on' **iCloud Photo Sharing**, in **System Preferences->iCloud->Photos** (select **Options** to see the iCloud photos preferences)

- Or Turn on this same feature from **Photos -> Preferences -> iCloud**

System Preferences->iCloud->Photos->Options

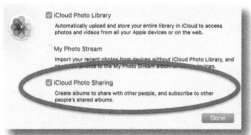

Photos -> Preferences -> iCloud

iCloud Photo Sharing

Having ensured that your iCloud Photo Sharing option is active, it is then easy to share a set of photos via your iCloud.

- Select one or more photos (using the technique described earlier)
- Choose the Share symbol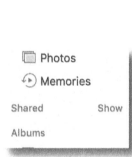
- Choose the option **iCloud Photo Sharing**
- Choose the shared iCloud album to which to add the photos – ie choose an existing Shared iCloud Album from the list shown or create a **New Shared Album**

- For a **New Shared Album**

  o In **Shared Album Name**, assign a name to the album,

  o In **Invite People**, enter the names of Contacts (they must be iCloud users who have also turned on the 'iCloud Photo Sharing' option). As you start typing a contact name, it will appear in 'blue' if the contact is on iCloud. Alternatively, choose the blue + to see your Contacts list and choose the applicable (and iCloud-enabled) Contacts. You can skip inviting people and do this later if your like.

  o Add a **Comment** if you like

  o Select **Create** after you have selected all the required contacts

Viewing Shared iCloud Photos

You can then view your Shared iCloud albums in the **Shared** area.

If you don't see anything listed in the Shared area, hover the mouse pointer over the word Shared so that the word **Show** appears, then click this **Show** option.

The Shared area of your Photos app shows those albums you shared with others and those that are shared with you.

iCloud Photo Sharing

The Activity option shows last added photos, comments and likes for all Shared Albums.

Permanently saving photos from a Shared iCloud Album

Photos you see in the Shared area are separate to those in the main Photos library. They are not permanently stored on your device and will disappear if the Shared Album is deleted or you 'unsubscribe' (see later in this section).

If you wish to permanently save photos that you have in the Shared area, you need to Import them to your Photos library.

Selected the Shared photos you wish to import (using the selection method described earlier in this guide).

Right Click (or two-finger-click) on one of the selected photos and choose **Import**.

Adding photos or videos to a Shared iCloud Album

To add new photos to a Shared iCloud Album, select the Shared album then choose **Add photos and videos**

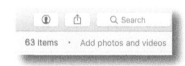

The Imported photos will then appear as the last few photos in your All Photos album (until you add more photos, that is).

Managing who can see your Shared iCloud Album

Add new subscribers to a Shared iCloud Album by choosing the 'Person' symbol at top right, visible when you select a Shared Album.

iCloud Photo Sharing

Change the name of the Shared album in the first field of the window that appears.

The + symbol in the 'Invite People' frame allows additional people to be invited to subscribe to the album.

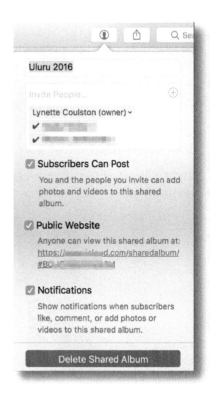

If there is someone you want to remove as a subscriber, just click the 'down-arrow' on the right of their name and choose the option 'Remove Subscriber'

You will see several other options in this screen

- Choose whether subscribers can add photos to the shared albums (**Subscribers can Post**)

- Choose whether you want **Notifications** popping up on your Mac about any activity in relation to album

- Option to create a '**Public Website**' that can be shared. This generates a link to a web page that will show your Shared iCloud Album's photos, a link that can be shared with those who don't use Apple or iCloud. Your iCloud album can then be viewed in any web browser using the shared link

Unsubscribing from an album someone else shared with you

If you no longer wish to see an iCloud Album that someone else shared with you, just right-click (or two-finger-click) on it and choose **Unsubscribe**.

This will remove the album from the Shared area on all your devices.

iCloud Photo Sharing

Special 'Family' Shared Album

If you are part of an iCloud Family, a special Shared iCloud Album automatically appears in the Shared list. It is called Family.

As you would guess, it is designed for sharing photos with other members of your iCloud Family,

You can't Delete or Unsubscribe from this Shared Album.

Deleting a Shared Album

If you no longer want to keep a Shared iCloud Album, right-click and choose **Delete**.

Alternatively, choose and select the **Delete Shared Album** option at the bottom of the window.

The Shared Album will be removed from the Shared area on all your devices.

Deleted shared albums also disappear from Shared area of any subscribers.

CPSIA information can be obtained
at www.ICGtesting.com
Printed in the USA
BVOW10s1519240817
492847BV00015B/186/P